M

by Tom Gato
illustrated by John Wallace

PEARSON

Glenview, Illinois • Boston, Massachusetts • Chandler, Arizona
Upper Saddle River, New Jersey

My name is Tom.
This is my street.
Gabe and Sam are my friends.
What can you see on my street?

The Barr family now lives on my street.
They have a dog named Max.
Look at my street.
What is new?

Now it is summer.
What is new on my street?
We like Mrs. Barr's garden!
Her son is named Dan.

Now it is fall.
What is new on my street?
Dan plays with us now.
Max plays with us, too.

Now it is winter.
It is cold.
Look at my street.
Can you tell what is new?

Now it is spring.
Look at my street.
We have a new playground!
We want to play all day.

Now it is summer.
We love the playground!
Look at my street.
Can you see the new things?